REX CONWAY'S
MIDLAND
STEAM JOURNEY
VOLUME TWO

THE HISTORY PRESS

First published in the United Kingdom in 2009 by
The History Press
The Mill, Brimscombe Port, Stroud, Gloucestershire, GL5 2QG

British Library Cataloguing in Publication Data
A catalogue record for this book is available from the British Library.

ISBN 978-0-7509-5128-9

Typeset in 10/12pt Palatino.
Typesetting and origination by
The History Press.
Printed and bound in England.

Contents

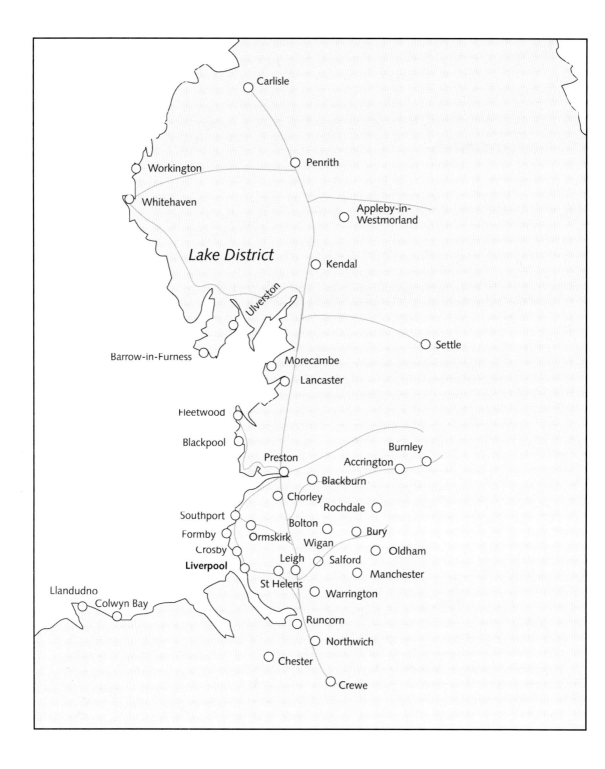

Carlisle

Workington

Penrith

Whitehaven

Appleby-in-
Westmorland

Lake District

Kendal

Ulverston

Settle

Barrow-in-Furness

Morecambe

Lancaster

Fleetwood

Blackpool

Burnley

Preston

Accrington

Blackburn

Chorley

Rochdale

Southport

Bolton

Bury

Formby

Ormskirk

Wigan

Crosby

Oldham

Leigh

Salford

Liverpool

Manchester

St Helens

Warrington

Llandudno

Colwyn Bay

Runcorn

Northwich

Chester

Crewe

Introduction

In volume one of my Midland Steam Journey we travelled from Bristol to Carlisle. At Sheffield we were joined by our other journey, which started at London St Pancras, and travelled along the picturesque Settle–Carlisle line to our final destination. Then we returned to London to catch a train to North Wales over the West Coast Main Line (WCML) via Manchester.

I soon realised that there were not enough pages in book one to cover the last part of the Midland Steam Journey from Crewe to Carlisle. There are so many important junctions, steam sheds and stations that we can visit from the West Coast Main Line, that I felt, with some justification, I would be criticised if I did not make the effort to search my archive for photographs taken in as many places as possible. After many hours of searching some 65,000 negatives, the midnight oil being burnt by the gallon, I found a considerable amount suitable to complete a second volume. Once again though, some had no information or a very brief note saying 'Wigan–Southport Line' or 'Near Carnforth'. I have tried to get accurate information, asking fellow enthusiasts and looking at countless books to try to identify backgrounds with some success. However, I will ask readers if they do spot mistakes, please not to be too critical. As I always say, every question is easy if you know the answer. The same is true with locations. They may be in your area and you will say 'But that's obvious it's . . .'. However, I am hundreds of miles away and I don't always know the answer, so I would appreciate being informed of the correct information, enabling me to correct my archive.

When you look at the map of the line from Crewe to Carlisle, it's only approximately 120 miles. However, in the first 60–80 miles it goes through more areas of steam sheds, stations and places of railway interest anywhere outside of London, which is why there had to be a second volume. From Crewe we shall be taking in Liverpool and the Fylde Coast, then on towards Manchester taking in Bolton, Bury, the works at Horwich and many other railway centres. Back on the West Coast Main Line we shall be at Preston with a junction to the holiday centre of Blackpool, Mecca for workers from the industrial towns of Lancashire. Beyond Preston we shall be travelling at speed to Carnforth. I would have made a pun and said 'A brief encounter', but that's a bit corny. On towards Oxenholme and then the Lune Gorge with names that every enthusiast knows: Dillicar with its troughs, to make sure engines have sufficient water to tackle the journey ahead; Scout Green and then Shap, a photographer's dream where 'Duchesses' battle unaided to the top of the bank with fifteen or more coaches. It was on this part of the WCML in 1936 that no. 6201 *Princess Elizabeth* topped the bank at 60mph with a test train. Over the top and we shall soon be at the end of our steam journey – Carlisle! Once again I hope you enjoy the trip with me, and we shall meet again on other journeys. If you have negatives gathering dust that can help me with further journeys, please contact me.

Rex Conway

9F 2–10–0 no. 92026, photographed near Crewe in 1957. This is one of the locos fitted with the experimental Franco-Crosti boilers with the chimney on the right-hand side, just in front of the cab. The normal chimney was blanked off. This experiment did not last very long.

No. 42476 2–6–4T Stanier, built in 1935, waits to leave Crewe. In the background is 'Royal Scot' no. 46152 *The Kings Dragoon Guardsman*.

Rex Conway's Midland Steam Journey

Our small band of steam enthusiasts have parked themselves on the platform trolleys which all spotters will remember being sometimes loaded with postal sacks, though more often with small boys with notebooks and the occasional group of older spotters, who prefer to be called enthusiasts or photographers. We are looking at photographs I have brought along for our group to look at and comment on before our train for Carlisle arrives. Everybody called in at the refreshment rooms to make sure they have drinks and sandwiches. The cameras are ready and we have plenty of film. There are some final comments on the photographs before we hear the loudspeaker announcing our train to Carlisle.

Another train waiting to leave Crewe, the 2P 4–4–0 no. 40660 at its head, with a 5A shed plate (Crewe North). It's on home ground.

The 'Royal Scot' class was introduced in 1927, built to a design by Fowler at Crewe.
As can be seen in these three photographs, they had large parallel boilers, small chimneys and
were well received by the LMS drivers. Some survived into British Railways in this form.

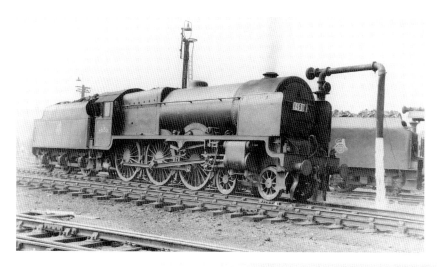

No. 46156 *The South Wales Borderer*, 1952.

No. 46140 *The Kings Royal Rifle Corps*, 1949.

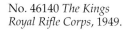

No. 46134 *The Cheshire Regiment*, 1949.

When William Stanier joined the LMS from the GWR (where he gained experience with taper boilers), he decided to re-boiler the 'Royal Scots' with a taper boiler and double chimneys. He turned a good locomotive into a superb locomotive, not only in performance but in looks too. My fellow travellers all shared my opinion. The conversation then turned to the train that would take us north. Several hoped we would have a 'Duchess' up front. Others, including myself, wanted a 'Royal Scot'.

No. 46119 *Lancashire Fusilier* as built by Stanier. The first conversion was in 1943, although he did experiment with no. 6170 in 1935 which was renumbered 6399 and named *Fury*. Regrettably, the boiler tubes exploded, bringing the experiment to a halt in 1949.

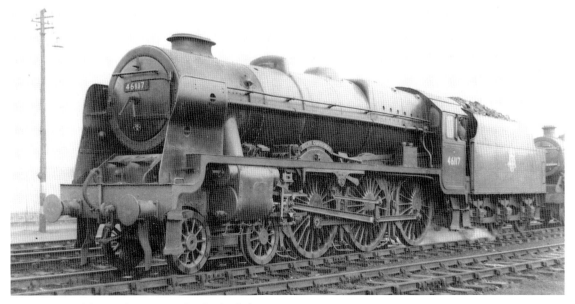

No. 46117 *Welsh Guardsman* in its final rebuilt form, 1953.

A 4–6–0 'Jubilee' no. 45610 changed its name. When it was built it was given the name *Gold Coast*, but this changed to *Ghana* when the Gold Coast gained independence in the 1950s. This photograph was taken at Crewe in 1949.

The one and only, Riddles design, no. 71000 *Duke of Gloucester*. There were going to be more of this class built, but before this could happen, the top brass at British Railways, no doubt on direction from the government, decided steam was to be phased out and that diesel was the way forward. As a result the *Duke of Gloucester* remained the only one of its class to be built. It was photographed here at Crewe when it was brand new.

The loudspeaker has announced our train approaching the platform. We hear the squeal of brakes being applied and into view comes a 'Royal Scot' at the head of our train. The engine stops just in front of us. You can imagine the scrabble to get into position to take our photographs. A gentle hiss of steam and the driver and fireman climb down from the cab to be relieved by a fresh crew who will take the train to Carlisle. It is an excited group of enthusiasts who board the train and find an empty compartment in the coach next to the engine, cameras at the ready and windows open, just in case we see something coming off the Chester line which branches off the WCML at the north end of Crewe station. Here we go! With a blast of steam on the hooter and that gentle tug that travellers behind steam engines know so well, and we are off on our journey to Carlisle.

Ready to leave Crewe for Carlisle is 'Royal Scot' no. 46110 *Grenadier Guardsman*.

Almost as soon as our train has cleared the platform on our journey, the Chester line branches left and the huge complex of Crewe Works comes into view. My fellow enthusiasts are crowded by the windows to get a photograph of the factory. Almost at the same point the right-hand side sees the Manchester line leave the WCML. Once past this complex of lines, things settle down and we are back in our seats. It's fairly straight now, so our 'Royal Scot' will be picking up speed through Winsford. We will soon be approaching the next point of interest, Hartford, where the Chester–Manchester line crosses over us, and continues through Northwich on its way eastward.

4–6–2 Pacific no. 46229 *Duchess of Hamilton* at the head of 'The Ulster Express' near Crewe, 1955.

Near Hartford, 3-cylinder Compound no. 40936 is double-headed with 'Royal Scot' no. 46168 *The Girl Guide*, 1955.

Northwich 9G is principally a freight engine depot. Its yard can be clearly seen from the station platforms. These three views are typical of the locos to be seen on shed.

A rather elderly 0–6–0 no. 43538, a Johnson Midland engine, that first saw service in 1885.

0–8–0 no. 49328 showing the station clearly in the background.

Introduced in 1927, here is a Fowler design, 2–6–4T no. 42386.

2–8–0 no. 48441, a Stanier-designed freight engine which was a great success with nearly 700 built, many seeing service overseas during the Second World War. This view is near Northwich, 1958.

Another lineside view near Northwich, this time 0–8–0, no. 49431 in 1954.

We have been travelling at a good pace. The sound of the 'Royal Scot's' exhaust through the open windows is music to our ears. We shall soon be approaching Preston Brook. Just before, to the left of our train, is Weaver Junction where the main line to Liverpool leaves. Our group starts chatting about the points of interest on the Liverpool line. We are told about the Weaver Viaduct which comes shortly after leaving the WCML. It was built in 1837 to a Joseph Locke design for the Grand Junction Railway. Constructed of red sandstone, it is 450 yards long with twenty arches – its highest point being some 70ft above ground.

4–6–0 'Black 5' no. 45303 near Preston.

After Weaver, the junctions come thick and fast: Runcorn, Widnes, Speke and many others. These two views came with limited information, only that they were in the Runcorn/Speke area. I would certainly be pleased to hear from anyone with more details.

'Class 5' 4–6–0 no. 45196. It has an 8A (Edge Hill) shedplate.

Another 'Class 5', 4–6–0 no. 44859.

Speke is another of those sheds that you would only find freight engines, and in large numbers. The shed is in a triangle of lines. The Allerton–Garston Docks and Ditton–Speke were popular places for spotting passenger trains going to Lime Street and a great number of freight going to and from the docks area of Liverpool.

4MT 2–6–0 no. 43028 was introduced in 1947 and designed by Ivatt. It was photographed at Speke in 1954.

Built by Stanier in 1933, this class was a smaller version of the 'Black 5' 4–6–0 and was also well-liked by the drivers. This view is of no. 42948 also at Speke, 1959.

The final stretch of line before Liverpool Lime Street passes Edge Hill shed 8A, which supplies locos for expresses out of Lime Street. It has a large compliment of named engines: favourites like the 'Princess Royals', 'Duchesses', 'Royal Scots', 'Jubilees' and many visiting engines. Edge Hill station, built in 1836, is close to the Olive Mount Cutting and Waterloo Tunnel, where trains were hauled up the incline by rope-winding engines A red-brick winding house is situated just behind the platforms at Edge Hill.

'Princess Royal' 4–6–2 no. 46210 *Lady Patricia*, photographed at Edge Hill shed in 1955.

A much earlier view at Edge Hill of a little boy with a big engine – no. 11115 – one of the massive 4–6–4Ts of the Lancashire & Yorkshire Railway in 1928.

'Royal Scot' no. 46110
Grenadier Guardsman at
Edge Hill in 1955.

'Class 5' no. 45019
awaiting its next duty at
Edge Hill in 1958.

The only information
I have on this loco is its
location – Liverpool – and
a date of 1957. It was built
in 1897 as a docks
shunter, so I presume the
photograph is taken
somewhere in the docks
area.

Liverpool's major station fronts onto Lime Street, hence its name. Its frontage is a huge hotel, built in the 1870s for the London & North Western Railway. It has 200 bedrooms and, for the year it was built, has quite lavish plumbing with thirty-seven flushing toilets and eight bathrooms. The train shed behind the hotel is equally impressive. The station has been rebuilt several times. There are two curved roofs, one of 220ft wide, the other 185ft wide. I first visited Lime Street in 1952, when I took this picture of 'Jubilee' no. 45581 *Bihar and Orissa*. My second view of the frontage was in 1955 when I marched down Lime Street in a Remembrance Day parade with the RAF.

Liverpool's second largest station is Exchange, which serves the Southport areas, as well as the line to Manchester via Aintree. The station was opened in 1850, jointly owned by the Lancashire & Yorkshire Railway, and the East Lancashire Railway. However, much bickering between the two companies resulted in the station having two of everything: two booking offices, two waiting rooms, two refreshment rooms and the list goes on. The station even had two names. The L&Y called it Exchange, while the ELR called it Tithebarn Street. Finally, in 1859, common sense prevailed and the companies amalgamated.

'Class 5' no. 44993 on its way north from Liverpool Exchange.

Bank Hall shed 27A was another of Liverpool's steam depots, servicing Exchange station and also the docks area.

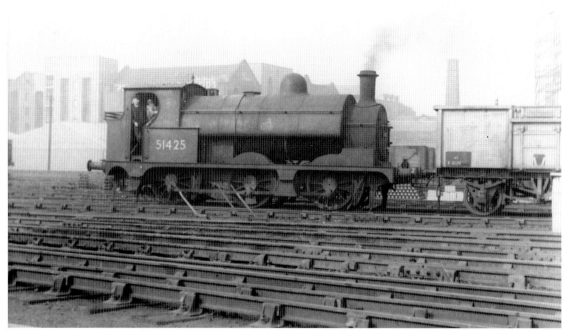

0–6–0T ST no. 51425 shunting at Bank Hall, 1953.

2–6–2T built to Stanier's design. No. 40168 is seen on Bank Hall shed, 1953.

Aintree, home of the Grand National, saw many specials arrive with thousands of visitors on race days. Aintree shed also had a large contingent of freight locos.

LMS no. 12405 on Aintree shed in 1934.

No. 52378, photographed in 1953 at almost the same spot as the picture above.

These two views of LNWR trains came with minimal information, briefly telling me it was taken on holiday when visiting Southport in 1913. It does not even necessarily mean the photographs were at Southport. I would appreciate hearing from anyone who can help with identification.

LNWR no. 2642.

LNWR no. 2270.

We have a positive I.D. for this photograph, Ansdell and Fairhaven near St Annes. This may have been taken on the same date as the previous pictures. This view is of LNWR no. 2621.

'Lancashire and Yorkshire electric train on the Southport line' reads the information with this negative. The display board reads 'All Stations to Hall Road' which is near Liverpool's Exchange station. The number on the side is 3022.

We have only scratched the surface of the interesting railway locations in the Liverpool area, but we must get back to Warrington to continue our journey to Carlisle. Just before Warrington are water troughs at Moore, so it's windows shut to make sure we don't get watered along with the engine. Then we are speeding through Warrington Bank Quay. One of our group tells us to lookout for Warrington 8B shed, which is about a mile north of the station on the left of our train. We may be able to get a photograph from the window, so once again, our cameras are ready.

Warrington 8B Shed with a 2–6–0. This class was commonly nicknamed the 'crabs'. Here we see no. 42849 on shed in 1963.

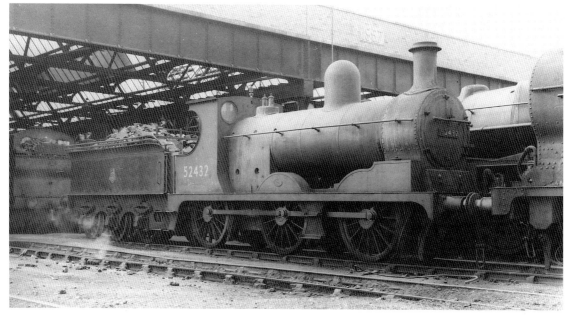

0–6–0 no. 52432, built in 1889 by Aspinall for the Lancashire & Yorkshire Railway.

Another view of Warrington shed when it was still under LNWR ownership. It is seen this time many years before the photograph opposite. A few chimneys had disappeared in the interim, but not a great deal really changed.

There are a maze of junctions in the Warrington area, and not far from Warrington the Liverpool–Manchester Line crosses the WCML at Newton-le-Willows. Here, 'Britannia' no. 70043 *Earl Kitchener* is near Newton-le-Willows. The Liverpool–Manchester is the original line where the Rainhill trials took place in October 1829, where the *Rocket* famously won. Equally well-known was the first case of someone being run over by a locomotive after the *Rocket* knocked down and killed the MP William Huskisson on the opening day of the railway.

Three views of locomotives at St Helens shed near Rainhill.

L&Y saddle tank no. 27337.

0–8–0 no. 49288 receiving its ration of coal at St Helens.

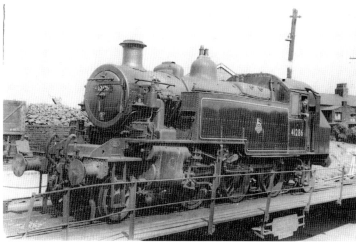

A more up-to-date view at St Helens is this photograph of 2–6–2T no. 41286 on the turntable.

One of our group is from Manchester and tells us about many of the locations he knows, although he couldn't help with the identification of this picture. The information on the negative packet was unreadable although the photograph was taken by someone living in Manchester.

This photo is of 'Britannia' no. 70044 *Earl Haig* with a full tender and 'The Mancunian' headboard. It would be likely, as it is at Manchester. It is backing down into the platform at London Road to take the train to London in 1954.

Two views near Manchester. It's very difficult to identify photographs in the country where there is nothing save for a fence or a lone bush. All I know, from limited information, is that they were taken near Manchester.

'Jubilee' class 4–6–0 no. 45582 *Central Provinces*, with the home signal only just raised. It is either approaching a junction or a station.

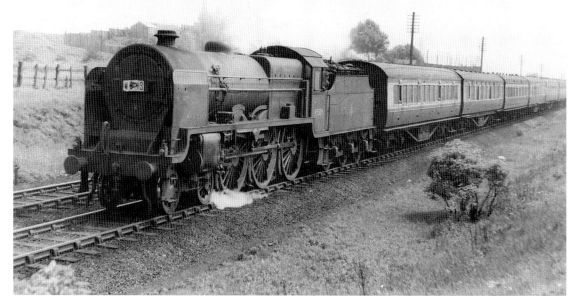

'Patriot' 4–6–0 no. 45519 *Lady Godiva*. Perhaps the buildings in the background will give a clue?

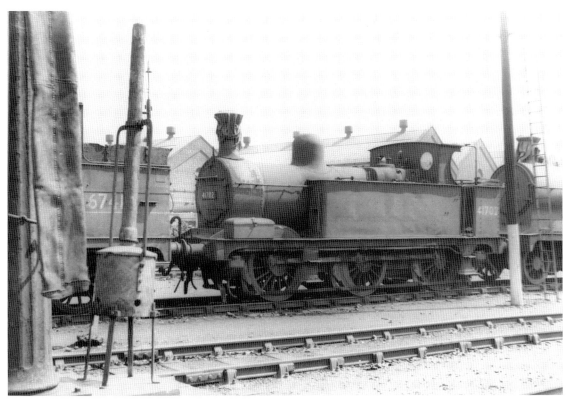

Gorton 9G is the setting for this photograph of 0–6–0T no. 41702, obviously in store, with the canvas over the chimney. It was very elderly, having been built in 1878 by Johnson of the Midland Railway.

4–4–0 3-cylinder Compound no. 41063, photographed at Trafford Park, Manchester.

I could never see the likeness of these locomotives to crabs, which was the nickname they had among the train spotters. They were more like workhorses (the Shire type that pulls the plough rather than the one that jumps over fences and races past the winning post). Designed by Hughes for the Lancashire & Yorkshire Railway, nearly two hundred and fifty were built. After the grouping in 1923, they were to be seen all over the LMS system.

2–6–0 5MT no. 42811 near Manchester with a freight train. The leading trucks are loaded with field guns, 1954.

No. 42886, another 'Crab' in the Manchester area, with a local stopping train, 1954.

Manchester Victoria and Manchester Exchange share a platform which is the longest in the country. Victoria station is one side of this platform and Exchange is on the other. It must be very confusing for travellers. Victoria was opened in 1844 for the Manchester & Liverpool Railway, and was later to become a Lancashire & Yorkshire station. In 1844 the London & North Western opened Exchange station right next door to Victoria, sharing the long platform. Manchester can boast of having the oldest railway station in the world, Manchester Liverpool Road. It was built by George Stephenson in 1830 and is still unaltered. This was the terminus of the Liverpool & Manchester Railway. It still retains warehouses from 1830, built to hold thousands of bales of cotton brought from Liverpool Docks to feed the mills in the Manchester area.

'Jubilee' Class 4–6–0 no. 45645 *Collingwood* at Manchester Exchange.

Back on the main line, (after a little trip down memory lane from one of our band of enthusiasts about locations in Manchester), we are now approaching the maze of lines that is Wigan.

0–6–0 3F no. 52387 hauls a freight train through Wigan, 1953.

Stanier 2–6–4T no. 42539, photographed in Wigan station.

Springs Branch shed 8F, the main shed in Wigan. It is principally a freight shed but passenger engines could also be seen there.

0–8–0 no. 49129 at Springs Branch shed.

2–6–0 no. 42856, Springs Branch.

Another view at Springs Branch showing the diversity of locos that could be seen. Here 2–6–2T no. 40087 is on view.

Another of the unnamed 'Patriots' visiting Springs Branch, 4–6–0 no. 45550.

It's a good job we have stocked up on goodies from the refreshment room at Crewe, as our 'Royal Scot' at the front will not be stopping until we get to Carlisle. There is a lot of chatter in our compartment about locos we have seen and photographs we have taken. We shall only know what they are like when we see the finished prints. We are through Wigan now, and will soon be approaching the junction for Southport.

'Duchess' class 4–6–2 no. 46222 *Queen Mary* on the main line just north of Wigan.

Near the same spot is 'The Royal Scot', headed by no. 46237 *City of Bristol*.

'Black 5' no. 45069 with a parcels train near Wigan.

An express freight near Wigan, headed by 'Crab' no. 42926.

From Wigan there is a direct line to Southport, well used by holiday traffic from the industrial north. It passes through Burscough Junction, where the direct line from Liverpool to Preston crosses over.

'Jubilee' 4–6–0 no. 45634 *Trinidad* on the Southport line with a parcels train, 1954.

Also on the Southport line not far from Wigan is 'Class 5' no. 45449, 1959.

Not far from Wigan is the Lancashire & Yorkshire works at Horwich; not to the size of Crewe, but still a vital works. Built for the L&Y in 1887, it completed its first loco in 1889, a small 2–4–2 tank engine built by Aspinall, no. 1008. By 1907, the works had completed its 1,000th loco. In January 1922 the L&Y was taken over by the LNWR but a year later the LNWR was amalgamated and became part of the LMS. During the Second World War the works built tanks as well as munitions for the war effort, so their contribution was invaluable. In 1952 the works built one of the first British Railway engines, no. 76000. The last loco left the works in 1957.

4–6–0 'Patriot' no. 45543 *Home Guard* north of Wigan, not far from Horwich, 1954.

Horwich works showing a line of locos under repair – all freight which the works mainly concentrated on.

Works narrow gauge system, *Wren*, used for moving mouldings and small parts from building to building within the large Horwich complex.

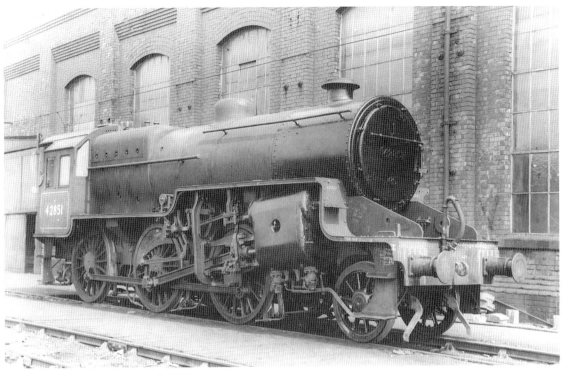

A loco that first saw life at Horwich, 'Crab' no. 42851.

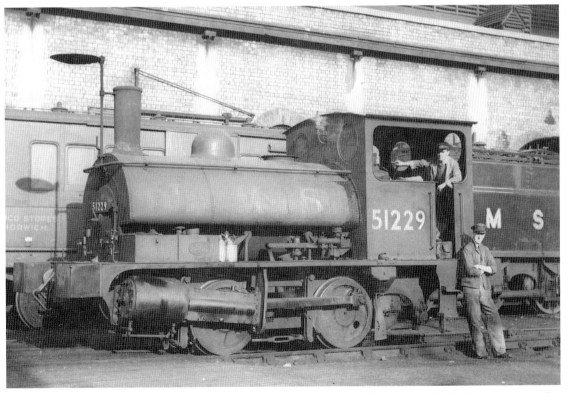

Another loco that first saw the light of day at Horwich is 0–4–0 saddle tank no. 51229. It was among the first of the engines built at Horwich, designed by Aspinall, in 1891.

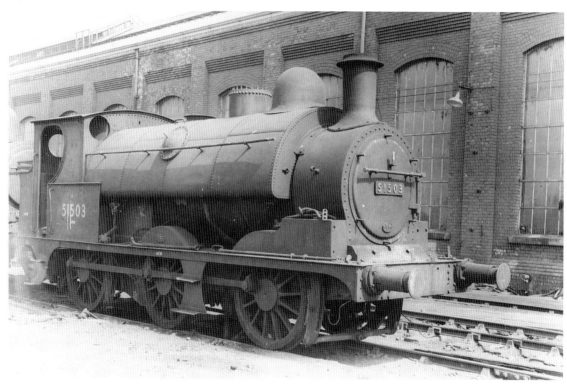

Another saddle tank produced at Horwich in the first few years was an Aspinall rebuild of a L&Y Barton Wright loco that was built in 1876. Weighing in at 42 tons it is twice the weight of the loco in photograph below.

0–4–0 saddle tank no. 51227 at Horwich.

From Horwich there is a junction – North goes to Euxton junction, while the WCML south goes to Lostock and Bolton.

2–6–4T no. 42291
photographed near Bolton.

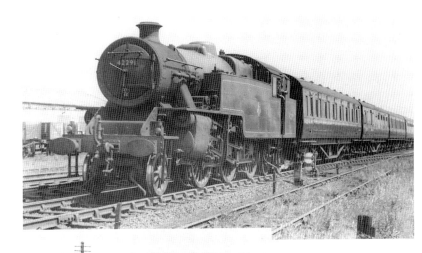

Stanier 2–6–0 no. 42952
on a freight train.

Inside Bolton shed is
2–4–2T no. 50647. This is
another L&Y loco designed
by Aspinall and built at
Horwich in 1889.

Bolton shed photographed on 3 August 1936. I don't know the shed, but from the angle of the picture, the photograph could be from a coaling tower.

Unnamed 'Patriot' 4–6–0 no. 45542. This was one of the few Patriots that became overlooked for naming. This view is near Bolton.

Bolton shed, deep in the heart of Lancashire's industrial mill country, was home to many freight engines. In particular were ex-Lancashire & Yorkshire engines, which had virtual monopoly in the early days of the twentieth century in the Lancashire area.

L&Y 0–6–0 no. 52139. A typical working loco in the mill areas built in 1889 and designed by Aspinall.

In later years after the grouping, LNWR locos – especially the 0–8–0 heavy freight engines, were to be widely seen in Lancashire. Here no. 49228 is photographed on Bolton shed.

0–6–0 saddle tank no. 51498, an L&Y Barton Wright of 1891, ready for duty at Bolton.

Stanier 2–6–4T No. 42653 on the main line near Bolton.

Simmering quietly on Bolton shed, another L&Y loco – no. 50850 built in 1892 – received several rebuilds. The first in 1898 gave it longer side tanks. Then in 1910 it received a Belpaire Boiler.

Photographed somewhere between Bolton and Bury is 'Jubilee' no. 45571 *South Africa*, 1959.

There are so many locations, sheds and stations in this area that we can only mention a few. We will start with Bury, a Lancashire & Yorkshire shed through and through.

Bury shed in the 1950s with an assortment of locos, including several Stanier tanks and a 'Crab'.

A typical L&Y 0–6–0 no. 52289.

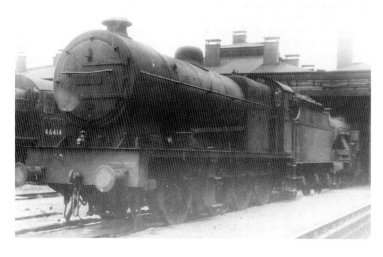

One of the large-boilered 0–8–0s introduced in 1929 to a Fowler LMS design, is no. 49667 on Bury shed, 1953.

Next comes Agecroft, a general view of the shed possibly from a coaling tower. This view is in LMS days, possibly the 1930s.

This view of Agecroft in 1958 has a good selection of locos on view – several WD 2–8–0s 'Black 5's, a tank and, of course, a 'Crab'.

A Lancashire & Yorkshire 'Pug', 0–4–0 saddle tank no. 51207 at Agecroft. It has a narrow wheelbase for working docks and small yards where there are severe curves.

These huge 4–6–4 tanks, designed by Hughes for the Lancashire & Yorkshire Railway, did not actually come out of the works until 1924. Weighing 100 tons and with 6ft 3in wheels, they were powerful-looking locos. This view is of no. 11111 at Agecroft shed in 1925.

0–8–0 no. 49508 in company with an 0–6–0 'Jinty' in the yard at Agecroft.

From Agecroft a line heads north to a Lancashire and Yorkshire stronghold, Accrington 24A, another freight depot serving the industry of northern Lancashire. These two views are somewhere on that line.

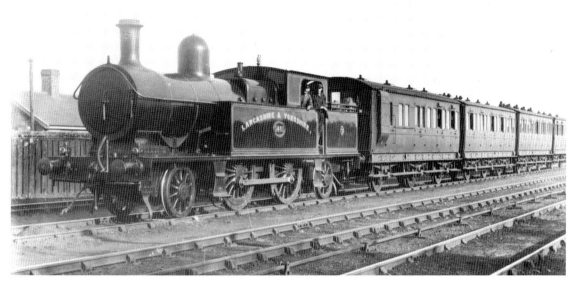

Lancashire & Yorkshire 2–4–2T no. 1461 with a rake of six-wheeled coaches and the L&Y name on the side tanks. This view dates from before 1923.

Many years later, in 1954, a Stanier 2–8–0 no. 48133 passes a signal-box with no visible name near Accrington.

Posing for the camera, the crew of 0–4–0ST no. 155 look rather glum, and obviously didn't respond to the cameraman's 'Smile, please.' The wording around the number 155 reads 'L and Y R Co. Makers Horwich 1901'. These locos became the 512xx 'Pugs' in British Railways ownership. This picture was taken at Accrington before 1923.

A difference in cleanness of 2–6–2T no. 41263. There was pride from the L&Y crews but sadly in BR ownership there were not enough staff for cleaning, and you couldn't expect the crew to clean engines after working long shifts.

A pre-war LMS view of Barton Wright 0–6–0ST no. 11484.

A 4–4–0 2P no. 40409 ready for duty on Accrington shed, 1953. Rebuilt in 1912 by Fowler, from an original design by Johnson for the Midland Railway, they had 7ft driving wheels.

LMS 0–6–0 no. 12606 was built originally in 1889, but was rebuilt in 1912 by Hughes of the L&Y. It became no. 52606 under British Railways ownership.

Fairburn 2–6–4T no. 42299 near Accrington, 1953.

Just before Blackburn is Mill Hill, with Compound no. 41091 on a local stopping train, 1954. These locos were built in 1924, a development of a Johnson design for the Midland.

Another L&Y shed devoted to freight is Lees 26F. From Oldham shed on view is 0–8–0 no. 49618. We are dodging around a bit now as we have got to get back to the West Coast Main Line. We will have a look at a few more locations.

'Jubilee' 4–6–0 no. 45581 *Bihar and Orissa*, one of the 'Jubilees' named after Indian States from the days when Queen Victoria ruled the British Empire. The naming took place in the 1930s. This photograph was taken at Blackburn at the head of an enthusiasts' special.

Todmorden station Up platform photographed from a train stopped at the Down platform in 1955. Not far from Todmorden is Gauxholme Viaduct, built for the Manchester & Leeds Railway in 1841. It was considered to be a great feat of engineering. The viaduct, built of stone and eighteen arches long, crosses a canal twice in a short distance.

'Royal Scot' no. 46117 *Welsh Guardsman* near Todmorden in 1961.

A bit further on towards Leeds is Sowerby Bridge. This photograph is of L&Y 0–6–0 no. 52400 in 1958.

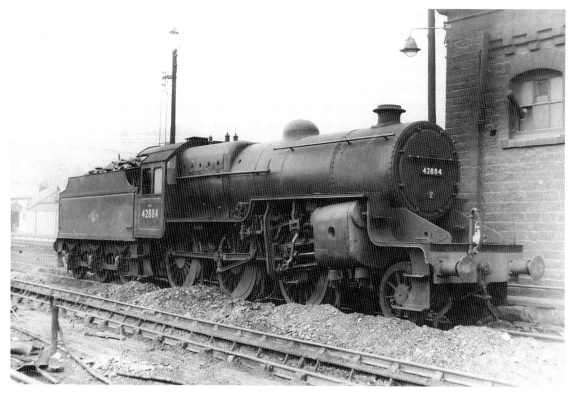

'Crab' 2–6–0 no. 42884 photographed in almost the same spot at Sowerby Bridge.

Three more views at Sowerby Bridge.

WD no. 90664 working its
way through Sowerby
Bridge with a freight train.

Ivatt 2–6–0 no. 46438
introduced in 1946 by the
LMS is photographed at
Sowerby Bridge in 1958.

'Jinty' 0–6–0 shunting at
Sowerby Bridge.

Three views of tank locomotives at Low Moor shed.

2–6–2T no. 41250 in the yard.

A Fairburn 2–6–4T no. 42107.

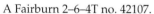

Another Fairburn, no. 42116.

We must start making our way back to the West Coast Main Line or we could well stay in the Lancashire area for the rest of the book. However, we will just mention a couple more. Huddersfield was a London North Western territory.

'Black 5' 4–6–0 no. 44914 near Huddersfield.

2–8–0 at Huddersfield back in LNWR days, c. 1915.

2–4–2T no. 50865 on shed, 1954.

Back on Lancashire & Yorkshire ground in Burnley, a viaduct dominates the town. Built in 1848 for the East Lancashire Railway, passengers enjoy a birds' eye view as the train approaches Central station.

0–8–0 no. 49511 at Burnley.

This photograph could be anywhere in Lancashire. The information is very brief, just 'Manchester area', but I like it because its no. 44444 is unique and the driver is happy to have his photograph taken.

L&Y 2–4–2T no. 50651 near Colne.

LMS 0–8–0 no. 9517 at Skipton.

Two photographs of Lancashire & Yorkshire engines with no identification regarding location.

L&Y 0–8–0 no. 628.

Hughes L&Y 3P 4–6–0 no. 1508.

I try to put old photographs in my books to test the skills of my readers.
Of these three photographs, I can only give the loco number, and hope that someone else
can tell me the rest.

L&Y no. 1112.

LNWR no. 2663.

LNWR *Engineer Manchester*.

Another couple of teasers for my fellow enthusiasts: LMS 'Royal Scot' no. 6151 *The Royal Horse Guardsman* with experimental smoke deflectors.

A Webb 2–4–2T no. 46757 – no other information.

One last picture before we are back on the WCML. This view is of the small terminus of Oxenhope, opened by the Midland Railway in 1867 as the Keighley & Worth Valley Railway. It is a small branch from the Bradford–Skipton line. Judging from the picture it is a bit out in the wilds. There are a few milk churns on the platform, but there is no life to be seen, not even a cow in the fields. At last we are on the main line just north of Wigan. We can relax, have a sandwich or two and a drink of lemonade. The line is fairly straight until we get to Preston.

4–6–2 no. 46228 *Duchess of Rutland* approaching Boars Head Junction. The sloping top to the smokebox is a legacy of its streamlined days.

At Boars Head Junction, the West Coast Main Line continues straight on, while the line in the foreground makes its way to Blackburn. One of our band told us about the signal-box on stilts although, at the speed our 'Royal Scot' passed it, we only saw a blur.

Another view of Boars Head signal-box with 'Duchess' 4–6–2 no. 46253 *City of St Albans* passing on its way to London.

Near Boars Head Junction is another 'Pacific', no. 46228 *Duchess of Rutland*.

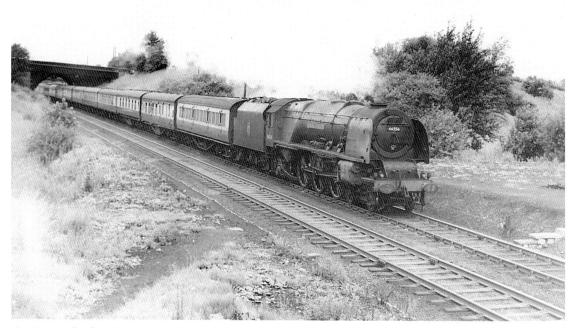

Again, not far from Boars Head is 4–6–2 no. 46256 *Sir William A. Stanier FRS*, named after the designer of these superb locos. As I am a Westcountryman, I take great delight in telling my fellow travellers that, of course, Stanier learnt his skills at the Great Western Works at Swindon and that his engines for the LMS incorporated a great many Swindon practices.

Our last view of Boars Head signal-box is of 'Jubilee' 4–6–0 no. 45678 *De Robeck* with an express heading south.

After passing the intensive railway system of Wigan with so many junctions and trains going in all directions and then roaring past Boars Head Junction, we have time to reflect on what has been seen so far. The chat in our compartment is about the locos, 'Duchesses', 'Scots', 'Jubilees', etc. – favourites of several of our group. Others liked the heavy freight engines; the 0–8–0s, and 2–8–0s. One could not stop talking about the old L&Y locos. We can now take a little more refreshment before Preston. We had better check our cameras and turn to a clean page in our notebooks as Preston is a busy centre.

4–6–2 no. 46205 *Princess Victoria*, on the WCML north of Wigan.

4–6–0 Patriot *Sir Robert Turnbull*, as rebuilt by Stanier. It's very difficult at a distance to tell them from a 'Royal Scot'. This photograph was taken somewhere near Leyland.

2–6–0 'Crab' no. 42763, north of Wigan.

We have now passed Euxton Junction and Leyland and will soon be at Farrington where there is a junction on the right with Lostock Hall shed, only a few miles from the WCML.

Rebuilt 'Jubilee' no. 5736 *Phoenix* without smoke deflectors at Farrington near Preston.

At the same spot is LNWR 'Claughton' no. 46004; the only survivor of the class to make it into British Railways ownership.

Lostock Hall 24C, another Lancashire and Yorkshire shed, mainly freight, situated just south of Preston on the line to Blackburn.

0–8–0 no. 49148 together with another 0–8–0 resting on Lostock Hall shed.

A heavyweight 0–8–0 no. 49315 introduced in 1912 and designed by Bowen Cooke for the LNWR.

No. 45196 'Class 5' 4–6–0. It has a 10A Wigan shed plate, so it's not far from home.

Another 'Class 5' not far from home is no. 45110. It carries a 10D Bolton shed plate.

We must not overlook the small locos that were at Lostock Hall. 0–4–0 saddle tank no. 47002 was photographed there.

0–6–0T commonly known as 'Jintys' no. 47427 dead on Lostock Hall shed.

Our train is slowing for our first stop, Preston. However, just before Preston is a junction off to the left to Southport, another line that the Lancashire & Yorkshire had a monopoly over. These two views are near Hesketh Bank. The first is in LMS days of 4–6–0 'Black 5' no. 4778 carrying a 24E shed plate. The second view is in BR days at the same spot. This time it's 2–6–4T no. 42481 with a three-carriage stopping train.

The brakes come on with a squeal and we come to a halt in Preston. It won't be a long stop, just time for a quick look around and a trip to the refreshment room. The original station was built in 1850. However, there were many problems so the various railway companies built other stations within the town causing more problems for the travelling public. Eventually the present station was built in 1880 jointly for the LNWR and the L&Y. This was told to us by a fellow enthusiast while waiting for service in the refreshment room. Out on the platform again we get a quick photograph of a passing freight, then it's back to our carriage. Almost as soon as we sit down, the guard's whistle sounds our departure. The 'Royal Scot' heading our train sounds the Stanier hooter, and we are off on the last, and perhaps most exciting, leg of our journey.

'Class 5' 4–6–0 no. 44822 at Preston.

'Jubilee' no. 45737 *Atlas* arriving at Preston.

'Class 5' no. 45373 making its way through Preston.

Another 'Class 5', no. 44902, at Preston with a long freight train.

Preston shed, with 'Royal Scot' no. 46166 *London Rifle Brigade* with a stable mate, 'Patriot' no. 45541 *Duke of Sutherland*.

We are leaving Preston and immediately we see the junction on our left for the favourite holiday destinations of workers from the industrial Lancashire towns and cities. It's this line that leads to the playgrounds of Lytham St Annes, its noisier neighbour Blackpool, and also to the fishing port of Fleetwood. Several of our group were enthusiastic about Blackpool, giving us chapter and verse on the fairgrounds and the tower.

'Class 5' 4–6–0 no. 45444 with a short parcels train at Preston.

Not long after leaving the WCML to head for Blackpool comes Lea Road water troughs. One can only guess at the number of trains using this route, especially during 'wakes week', as the holiday period in the summer was known. Four tracks wide with troughs on each, a signalman's job must have been non-stop.

LMS 0–6–0 no. 3480 does not look as if it is taking water on the Lea Road troughs, 1924.

L&Y 2–6–2 no. 24 is most certainly taking water, as is evident from the fireman leaning out of the cab watching the water spill by the trailing wheel. Another express can be seen approaching on the left.

Looking the other way at Lea Road, two LMS 0–6–0s, (nos 12252 and 12528), are on the troughs. The lead engine is obviously not thirsty but the second is being watered. This photograph was taken on 21 June 1924.

After Kirkham comes the junction on the left for St Annes on Sea. After passing Lytham, the main line runs past the sand dunes by the edge of the sea.

4–6–0 'Class 5' no. 44932 passing the sand dunes 1951.

'Jubilee' no. 45695 *Minotaur* passing the same point in 1951.

2–6–4T no. 42153, again with the same fence and sand dunes in view, 1951.

A short train of only three coaches with 4–4–0 3-cylinder 'Compound' no. 40937 in charge, 1951.

LMS 0–6–0 no. 4545 in St Annes station. Is someone climbing in or out of the first carriage trying to dodge paying, I wonder?

Just after the junction for St Annes comes the junction for Blackpool Central. The line carries on to Poulton, where it diverges south to Blackpool and north to Fleetwood.

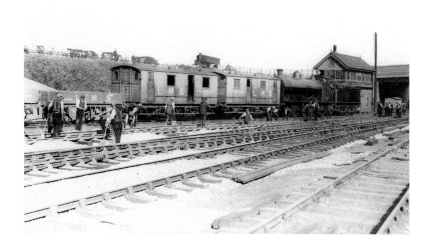

LMS engineer's train , with an 0–8–0 in charge relaying track near Poulton no. 1 signal-box, *c*. 1926.

Pounding past Poulton no. 2 signal-box is LMS 0–6–0 no. 4476 in 1928.

Lancashire & Yorkshire no. 15, approaching Poulton Curve Halt in 1920. There were only eighteen of these steam rail motors built in 1906.

Just before Fleetwood is Wyre Dock, the terminus for the steam rail motors. This view dates from the 1920s.

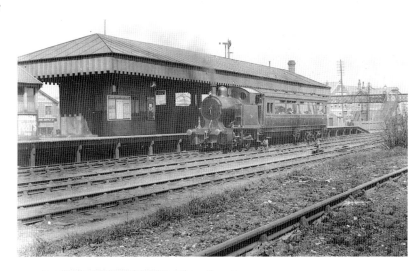

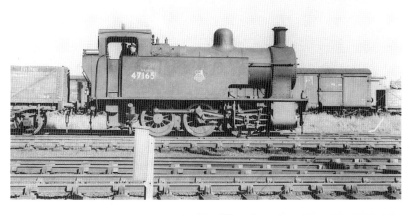

Introduced in 1928, this Fowler-designed 0–6–0T narrow wheelbase loco was built especially for dock working. This picture is of no. 47165 shunting at Fleetwood.

0–6–0ST no. 51419, older and bigger than the previous picture, was built in 1891 and, although roughly the same weight, the wheelbase is longer and would not get round the curves that no. 47165 could.

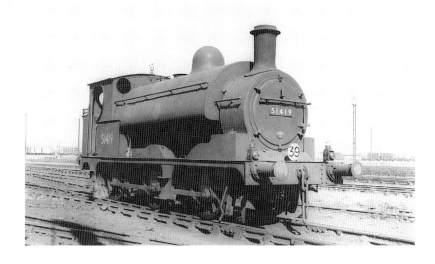

From Poulton it is just a short distance on the line that heads south-west to Blackpool North.

If you have a head for heights you can get a wonderful view of Blackpool Central station. This view was taken in 1952.

L&Y 4–6–0 no. 50455 was one of the Lancashire & Yorkshire passenger locos built by Hughes in 1921 which survived into British Railways ownership. Its L&Y number was 10455. It was withdrawn in 1951 and is photographed in that year heading an enthusiasts' special to York via Manchester at Blackpool.

'Jubilee' 4–6–0 no. 45653 *Barham*, which was named after one of the heroes of the Battle of Trafalgar, is seen on Blackpool shed.

On the turntable at Blackpool in LMS days is 'Jubilee' *Achilles* in 1938.

'Class 5' 4–6–0 no. 44744 was introduced in 1948. One of the Caprotti-fitted locos, it is possibly making its way back to the WCML, 1956.

We have heard all about the joys of Blackpool: the Tower, the Big Dipper, 'kiss me quick' hats and so on, from a couple of our enthusiasts while we have been eating sandwiches and drinking lemonade, but our train is now picking up speed. Time once more to take stock as we shall soon be into one of the most exciting parts of our journey, the Lune Gorge and Shap. But first we shall be over Brock Troughs, so, windows firmly closed.

LMS 0–6–0 no. 8134, a Webb LNWR coal engine built in the 1880s, is taking water on Brock Troughs in the 1920s.

A bit later, in 1930, is another view of Brock Troughs, this time with a 'Royal Scot' in original form – 4–6–0 no. 6119 *Lancashire Fusilier*.

Still on Brock Troughs, though this time with the 'Princess Royal' class no. 46202, the *Turbomotive* built in 1935. It was an experimental engine by Stanier and had two turbines. The one on the left in the picture is the large turbine for forward motion. On the other side is a smaller turbine for reversing. It received a double chimney from the start. It was a very capable engine and, but for the Second World War bringing experiments to a halt, many more may have been built. Finally it appeared from Crewe Works as a 'Princess Royal' no. 46202 *Princess Anne* early in 1952. Regrettably it had a very short life, being totally destroyed in the Harrow crash in October 1952.

'Royal Scot' no. 46114 *Coldstream Guardsman* has finished its drink, and is just coming off Brock Troughs in 1956.

We are speeding along now and the windows are open once more after Brock Troughs. The scenery is very rural but our film must be kept for railway views. Our 'Royal Scot' hooter sounds a long blast and, with our carriages swaying, we roar through Garstang Junction for the Garstang and Knott End Railway. Then we are on our way through Scorton and Bay Horse. It won't be long before we slow to a more leisurely speed to go through Lancaster.

2–8–0 no. 48133 near Garstang.

'Royal Scot' no. 46108 *Seaforth Highlander* near Garstang.

'Jubilee' 4–6–0 no. 45556 *Nova Scotia* on the WCML.

'Class 5' no. 44839 on the WCML.

Another view on the WCML. This time we see 'Jubilee' 4–6–0 no. 45556 *Nova Scotia*.

Bay Horse station, which L&NW opened in June 1840.

Another view of the West Coast Main Line with a clean 'Royal Scot' no. 46123 *Royal Irish Fusilier* at full speed, 1954.

Another sunny day on the WCML as 'Jubilee' class 4–6–0 no. 45633 *Aden* heads a southbound express.

A double-headed ballast train near Lancaster. The lead engine is 8F 2–8–0 no. 48062 and BR 2–6–0 4MT is the train engine.

'The Royal Scot' headed by 'Duchess' class 4–6–2 no. 46224 *Princess Alexandra* near Lancaster, 1954.

3-cylinder Compound 4P no. 41102 on Lancaster shed 11E.

'Royal Scot' 4–6–0 no. 46108 *Seaforth Highlander* on the WCML near Lancaster with a fitted freight train.

At Lancaster there is a junction on the right built by the Midland Railway that connects the WCML with the Carlisle & Settle line at Settle Junction. It goes by way of Hornby, Clapham and Giggleswick. Shortly after this junction is another to Morecambe on the left, where we are told by one of our band, who seems to have a liking for cockles, that Morecambe Bay supplies vast quantities of these little creatures for the restaurants and chip shops. Next comes Hest Bank and then Carnforth where we will slow for the curves past the station.

LMS 'Royal Scot' 4–6–0 no. 6165 *The Ranger (12th London Regt)* near Hest Bank in 1938.

Near Hest Bank a fitted freight train with 'Jubilee' no. 45589 *Gwalior* supplying the power. A couple of cows in the background seem uninterested.

An early photograph of an LMS 4–4–0 2P at Settle, probably taken in the early 1920s. It is no. 455 running light engine through the station.

Bridge rebuilding at Long Preston near Hellifield. 'Midland' 2–4–0 no. 209 is passing through slowly, watched by workmen, *c*. 1920.

We shall soon be approaching Carnforth station, built in 1846 for the Lancaster & Carlisle line with later extensions for the London & North Western and also the Furness Railway (FR). The Furness Railway platform and line diverge to the left to Barrow and to the right through to Whitehaven. There are also junctions to the Lakes. For Windermere and Coniston, the FR line also goes through Ravenglass, where of course, there is the narrow gauge Ravenglass & Eskdale railway. Back at Carnforth our train will be going through on the West Coast Main Line which curves away to the right. It is at this point that the conversation turns to the black and white film of Celia Johnson and Trevor Howard that put Carnforth on the railway enthusiasts' map. It's a romantic film called *Brief Encounter* but, to the enthusiast, the romance was supplied by the station setting with views of LMS locos running in and out.

The approach to Carnforth station from the south, 1930s.

Unrebuilt 'Patriot' no. 45543 *Home Guard* near Carnforth.

2–6–0 'Crab' no. 42926 near Carnforth.

'Class 5' 4–6–0 no. 45386 with an 11B Barrow shed plate near Carnforth.

We are going a long way back in time for this view of Carnforth shed, c. 1925.

The 'Royal Scot' express near Carnforth with no. 46230 *Duchess of Buccleuch* at the head.

'Class 5' no. 45086 near Carnforth.

0–6–0 no. 44501 in Carnforth station.

Looking at a railway map of the Furness to Whitehaven Line, it shows there are not many long straight stretches so one cannot expect a fast run. After leaving Carnforth, the first station the train arrives at is Silverdale. Then there is Arnside where there is a junction and a short stretch of line heads back to the WCML, while the Furness line crosses a bridge to Grange-over-Sands.

A Stanier 8F 2–8–0 no. 48126 near Silverdale.

The 'Class 5' 4–6–0 was a very common sight on the Furness route. This is no. 45427 at Arnside.

A photo of Arnside station, opened in 1858 by the Furness Railway. We can clearly see the junction back to the WCML.

Grange-over-Sands station was built in the same year as Arnside, but rebuilt in 1877 to a much grander scale.

Leaving Grange-over-Sands, the line skirts the coast of Morecambe Bay, then a short distance on through Clark and Cartmel, an inlet from the bay is crossed by a bridge near Lonsdale Cross. Almost immediately comes the junction on the right to Windermere Lakeside followed by Ulverston. There are a number of wayside stations and branch lines before the train runs into Barrow.

Furness Railway no. 103, photographed at Windermere Lakeside in 1919.

Another view in Furness Railway times of no. 111 picking up passengers at Ulverston in 1919.

Still in Furness Railway days is this view of 0–6–0 no. 66, a Sharp Stewart loco built between 1866 and 1870. It was photographed in Barrow Yards, *c*. 1920.

Another early view, this time of Furness Railway 2–4–2T no. 74 in Barrow, *c*. 1920. Originally built in 1875 as a 2–4–0, it was rebuilt in 1891.

Another Sharp Stewart 0–6–0 no. 81, built for the Furness Railway. This view is in Barrow, *c.* 1919.

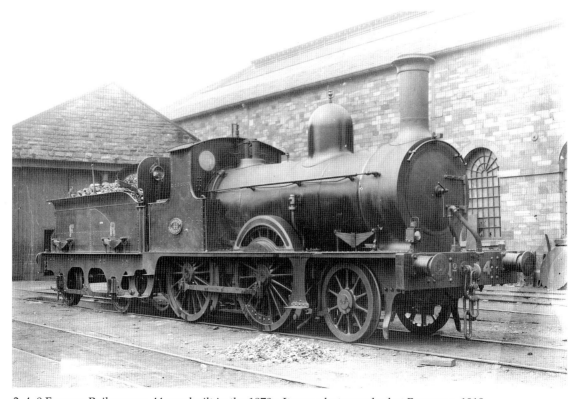

2–4–0 Furness Railway no. 44 was built in the 1870s. It was photographed at Barrow, *c.* 1919.

Leaving Barrow behind, the line once more runs near the coast of Morecambe Bay, this time through Kirkby and then Foxfield, where the junction for Coniston branches right. Opened in June 1859 as Coniston Lake by the Furness Railway, it was a very popular tourist attraction for the Victorian middle classes and the railway delivered them to hotels on the banks of the lake.

Coniston station, showing the attractive design of the overall roof and the lattice work of the over bridge.

The turntable and tiny shed adjacent to Coniston station.

Coniston station looking south.

Coniston station looking north showing the mountain towering above.

After Foxfield, another bridge crosses an inlet from Morecambe Bay. The Furness line then follows the coast to Ravenglass where the narrow gauge line to Eskdale branches from the main line.

Ravenglass station was opened in 1849 by the Furness Railway.

River Irt, one of the narrow gauge locos that work the Ravenglass and Eskdale Railway.

Back to the West Coast Main Line now. Excitement is building in our compartment as we have just left Carnforth and we are on the last leg of our journey. Only two of our group have been on this route before and tell us what it is like to roar into the Lune Gorge with the engine working hard to tackle Shap. The line was built for the Lancaster & Carlisle Railway by Joseph Locke who did not like building tunnels so the line follows the natural curves of the landscape, resulting in few straight parts and several severe gradients of which Shap is the most challenging to locomotives. Before Shap our 'Royal Scot' will be picking up water from Dillicar Troughs. Then the regulator will be wide open, and we shall get the full blast of the exhaust from our double-chimneyed 'Scot'.

'Jubilee' 4–6–0 no. 45619 *Nigeria* is building up speed before entering the Lune Gorge, 1951. Judging by the direction of the exhaust from the chimney it must have been a windy day.

4–6–0 no. 45599 *Bechuanaland* on the WCML north of Carnforth.

'Royal Scot' no. 46105 *Cameron Highlander* between Carnforth and Oxenholme.

One of our band of enthusiasts starts reminiscing about the streamlined Pacifics that worked over the WCML before the war. He dreamed of watching them storm up Shap with 'The Royal Scot' train. Like a magician, I reached into my bag and extracted a number of postcard photographs. Included in the selection were two views of 'Streamlined Coronations' on the WCML, not Shap, but enough to get everyone in our compartment excited.

LMS 4–6–2 no. 6222 *Queen Mary* taking water on Brock Troughs with 'The Royal Scot' train.

Another view of a 'Streamlined Coronation' no. 6221 *Queen Elizabeth* with 'The Royal Scot'.

We are travelling at good speed behind our 'Royal Scot'. We have the windows open, the sun is shining, and we shall soon be onto the approaches to Shap. But before then we will be passing through Oxenholme where there is a short branch left to Windermere.

'Patriot' no. 45537 *Private E. Sykes V.C.* pauses at Oxenholme with a freight train. It looks as though it is receiving a bit of attention.

Passing Oxenholme no. 2 signal-box, is 'Duchess' 4–6–2 no. 46237 *City of Bristol*.

Oxenholme station looking a bit deserted under a sky that suggests rain is not far away.

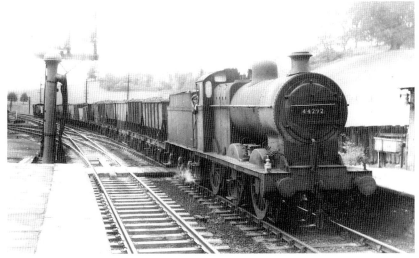

Bringing life to Oxenholme station on the same day as the previous view is 0–6–0 no. 44292.

Windermere station on a wet and dreary day. 'Class 5' no. 44927 looks as though it would much prefer to be in a nice warm shed.

Stanier 2–6–4T no. 42613 at Oxenholme with a Windermere train.

Back in LMS days, 2P Compound 4–4–0 no. 908 and an unidentified 2P near Grayrigg, *c*. 1938.

Low Gill station. This is a junction point of the WCML with a line to Clapham and eventually Settle.

'Royal Scot' 4–6–0 *British Legion* on the West Coast Main Line.

4–6–0 'Jubilee' no. 45719 *Glorious* with a southbound express near Tebay.

The windows in our carriage are open and everyone is trying to get a photograph from the window of our 'Royal Scot', picking up speed to attack the famous Shap Bank. We shall not be stopping for a banker at Tebay as many, especially freight, trains do. Tebay shed houses a number of Fowler and Stanier 2–6–4Ts for the purpose of banking. There is also a junction at Tebay to Kirkby Stephen and Darlington, which means some Eastern engines make an appearance. We are now approaching Tebay. One of our members who has travelled this route before, tells us Tebay shed 11D is on the left-hand side of our train. A stampede takes place to get to the corridor windows, sandwiches and drinks to be consumed before Shap left on our seats. I don't think many of our photographs taken at this point are going to be prize-winners as we are travelling at a fair speed and there are many obstacles between us and the shed.

No. 40636 class 2P 4–4–0 and an unidentified 'Royal Scot' pass through Tebay station. The shed can be seen in the background.

4–4–0 2P no. 40684 and an unidentified 'Class 5', building up speed through Tebay station.

Waiting its next call to banking duty at Tebay shed is Fowler 2–6–4T no. 42404.

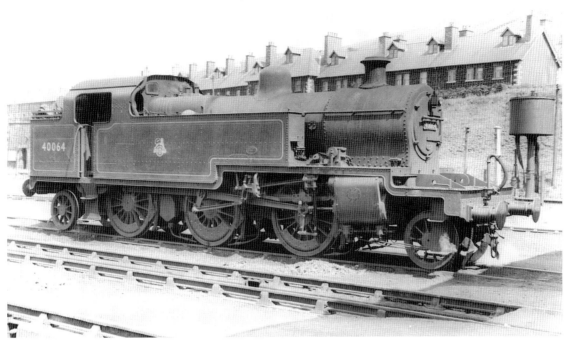

Another Fowler awaiting the call at Tebay is no. 40064. This time it's the smaller version of the previous picture. Being a 2–6–2T it has a smaller coal bunker.

Another 2–6–4T Fowler loco no. 42396 simmering quietly on Tebay shed.

Unnamed 'Patriot' 4–6–0 no. 45508 coasting through Tebay with a fitted freight. Putting a stovepipe chimney to this locomotive has, in my eyes, ruined the appearance of this engine.

Building up speed for the ascent of Shap, is 'Clan' 4–6–2 no. 72002 *Clan Campbell* introduced in 1952. It was not as successful a design as the 'Britannias'.

On a cold and wintry day, 'Jubilee' 4–6–0 no. 45556 *Nova Scotia* makes a spirited start from Tebay. No doubt the crew are keeping themselves warm with a roaring fire. Steam pressure is high as the safety valve has lifted, but the snowy conditions will be worse on Shap, so a good head of steam is essential.

As previously mentioned, there is a junction at Tebay to Kirkby Stephen station. This photograph was taken at Kirkby Stephen on the occasion of an enthusiasts' visit.

Arriving at Tebay with a train from Kirkby Stephen station, is 2–6–0 2MT no. 46475, piloting an Eastern region loco.

We are through Tebay now and the exhaust from our 'Royal Scot' is echoing back from the hills. A voice from one of our band tells us that the climb from Tebay is about 4 miles at 1:75 and the regulator will be pretty well wide open. We shall probably be doing about 75mph. There is no thought of finishing our sandwiches now with heads out of windows and cameras strapped safely around necks to try once more, to get an effect of smoke and steam from our 'Royal Scot' on Shap.

'Coronation' class 4-6-2 no. 46225 *Duchess of Gloucester* leaving Tebay with fifteen coaches on and no banker. It is at the head of 'The Midday Scot'.

Near Dillicar is 'Royal Scot' no. 46159 *The Royal Air Force*.

'Princess Royal' class no. 46209 *Princess Beatrice* taking water on Dillicar Troughs.

Hard at work, 4–6–2 no. 46229 *Duchess of Hamilton* is taking water from Dillicar Troughs while attacking the 1:75 of Shap. This setting is a railway photographer's dream.

Scout Green was another favourite spot for railway photographers. Here is 'Patriot' 4–6–0 no. 45542 – one of the unnamed of the class.

'Class 5' no. 45057 piloting an unknown 'Jubilee', descending Shap with a southbound express.

British Railways 'Class 5MT' introduced in 1951. No. 73055, with ten coaches, makes a fine picture on Shap.

Even an 0–6–0 with one truck and a guard's van should not find Shap too hard a task.

Stanier 2–6–4T with a four-coach train on Shap.

At the same spot on the same day, is 'Class 5MT' no. 44735.

Not far from Tebay on the ascent of Shap, is 'Princess Royal' class no. 46206 *Princess Marie Louise*.

'Royal Scot' no. 46128 *The Lovat Scouts* with a dry stone wall in the foreground – a characteristic view of Shap.

One of the last 'Royal Scots' to be rebuilt, no. 46156 *The South Wales Borderer*, again with a dry stone wall adding to the photograph.

Shap has supplied many a photographer with superb pictures in all conditions, and I am sure all enthusiasts will enjoy looking at a large selection of photographs taken at many vantage points on the 4 miles of the famous bank.

Descending the bank with a Glasgow–Blackpool holiday express, is 'Jubilee' no. 45742 *Connaught*.

Ascending Shap on the same day is another 'Jubilee' no. 45595 *Southern Rhodesia*.

Nearing the top of the bank is 'Jubilee' 4–6–0 no. 45593 *Kolhapur*.

Working hard is rebuilt 'Patriot' no. 45526 *Morecambe and Heysham*.

Who could wish for a better spot to have a picnic? Quietly eating your cold chicken sandwiches (or whatever else is in your picnic hamper), with the birds twittering, you suddenly hear it; the distant sound of an engine working hard. You pick up the camera, check the exposure, while all the time the exhaust is getting louder. With a roar it is past and, with the sound receding, you have your photograph. In this instance it is no. 46228 *Duchess of Rutland* on its way to Carlisle.

Over the top, the crew of no. 45571 *South Africa* can now relax for a while as they pass the Shap summit signal-box.

Shap station with four young spotters very close to the platform edge. Perhaps the signalman in the box will warn them when a train is approaching.

Another view of Shap station.

I promise our small band that I shall now finish the pictures at Shap. It has been a little bit of self-indulgence. I like looking at pictures of named locos working hard, and where better than Shap?

'Jubilee' no. 45657 *Tyrwhitt* passing through Shap station.

This time it's a 'Duchess' 4–6–2 no. 46241 *City of Edinburgh* working through Shap station.

It's with a mixture of excitement and sorrow that we settle back on the cushions in our compartment; excitement with the experience of climbing Shap behind a 'Royal Scot' working hard, and sorrow that it's all over. No doubt other passengers on the train look at our activities and wonder what our excitement is all about. They look out of the windows at the scenery and then return to reading their magazines and newspapers while our compartment is full of talk about Shap. We are now into the final few miles of our journey before Carlisle. It's time to finish our sandwiches and look forward to the next station of interest, Penrith.

A 'Class 5' making its way through Penrith with an express freight train.

Penrith shed 12C is home to some elderly locos that can be found on the line from Penrith to Workington via Keswick. Workington is quite an industrialised area with a number of branch lines, including one to Maryport.

LNWR Webb 'Cauliflower' 2F 0–6–0 no. 58412 built in about 1880. It is seen here in Penrith shed.

Another 'Cauliflower' at Penrith, no. 58409.

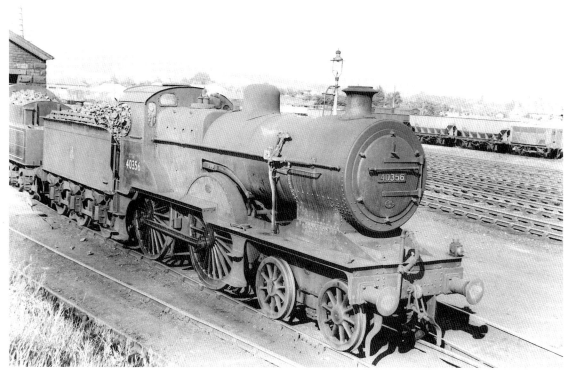

2P 4–4–0 no. 40356 in the yard at Penrith shed. Introduced in 1912, they have 7ft wheels.

'Patriot' 4–6–0 no. 45503 *The Royal Leicestershire Regiment* working its way through Penrith with an express freight.

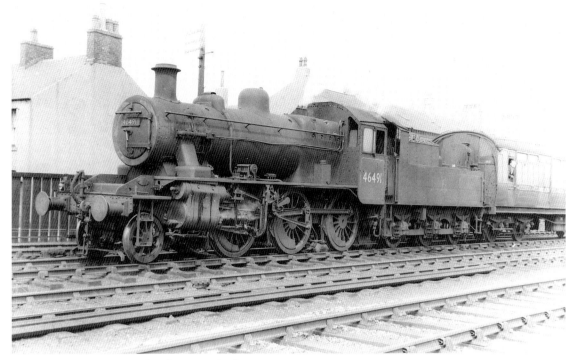

2–6–0 2MT no. 46491 on a local train at Workington.

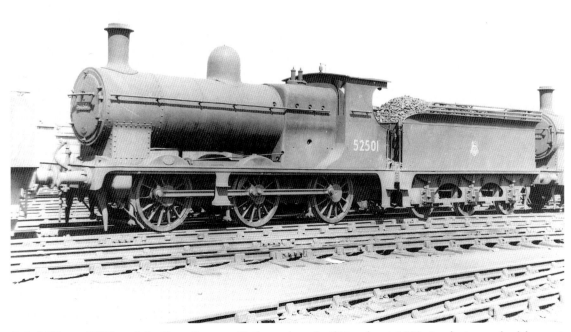

0–6–0 3F no. 52501, originally a Furness Railway loco built in about 1889, is photographed here at Workington.

0–6–0 no. 52499, also an ex-Furness Railway loco, at Workington.

Workington no. 2 signal-box.

The details that came with this photograph were 'no. 46247 *City of Liverpool* at Keswick'. It is carrying a single lamp on top of the smokebox which signifies a local stopping train or branch line train. It seems to be a large loco for working a branch. Perhaps it's a regular working, I would be interested to have this confirmed.

Leaving Penrith in LNWR days is no. 2645. It was an experiment class built by Whale in about 1906. At the grouping (1923), it became LMS no. 5532 *Britomart*.

'Class 5MT' 4–6–0 no. 45415 on the West Coast Main Line near Penrith.

It won't be long now before we reach Carlisle, where a variety of locos can be seen; from the express passenger locos to the small 0–6–0 tanks, as well as engines from the Scottish region.

Pickergill Caledonian 4–4–0 3P No. 54507 photographed at Carlisle Kingmoor Shed, 1953.

'Duchess' 4–6–2 class no. 46256, carrying the name of its designer, *Sir William A. Stanier FRS*, on the turntable at Carlisle Upperby.

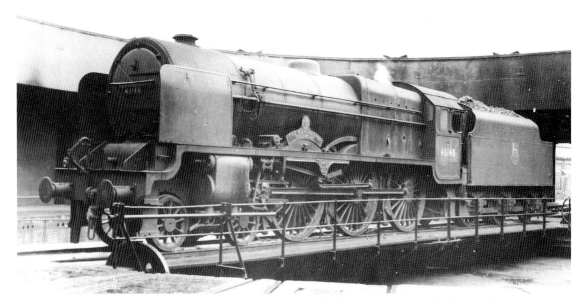

Another view of the turntable at Carlisle Upperby shed. This time unrebuilt 'Royal Scot' no. 46148 *The Manchester Regiment* is being turned.

Unnamed 'Patriot' 4–6–0 no. 45510 on shed.

As these two views show, Carlisle Upperby shed was not just for express passenger engines.

This is 0–6–0 tank engine no. 47391 on Upperby shed. These engines were nicknamed 'Jintys'.

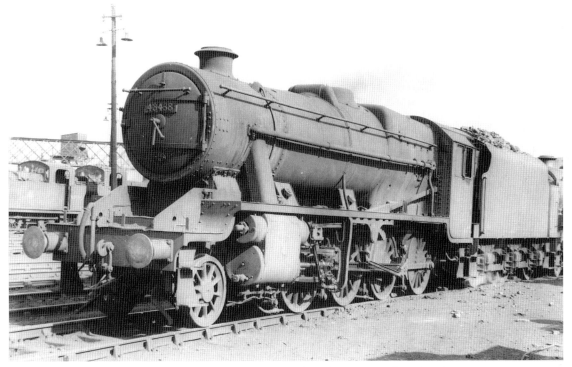

Stanier 2–8–0 freight engines could also be seen at Upperby. This view is of no. 48438.

Two more views at Carlisle Upperby.

'Jubilee' 4–6–0, a Manchester engine, no. 45702 *Colossus*.

Unnamed 'Patriot' 4–6–0 no. 45551.

Two views at Carlisle's other principle shed – Kingmoor.

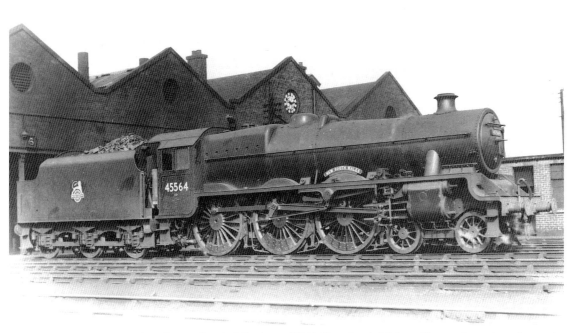

Judging by the coal piled in the tender, 'Jubilee' no. 45564 *New South Wales* will soon be out on the main line again.

Another 'Jubilee' at Kingmoor, no. 45579 *Punjab*.

Our journey is almost over. The 'Royal Scot' at the head of our train has slowed to not much more than walking pace. We have collected our cameras and note books and are ready to open the doors to get on to the platform to take those last few photographs.

Maryport and Carlisle Railway no. 18 leaving Carlisle in 1919.

Workington 12D 4–4–0 2P no. 40694 preparing to leave Carlisle Citadel station with a local stopping train to Workington.

Carlisle was an exchange station for both crews and engines.

'Royal Scot' no. 46165 *The Ranger (12th London Regt.)* waiting in the centre road at Carlisle to relieve a southbound crew and engine.

Another loco waiting to relieve a southbound train. This time it's a 'Duchess', 4–6–2 no. 46252 *City of Leicester.*

We are now approaching the platform at Carlisle Citadel which takes it's name from the law courts built just across the square from the station in 1810. The courts in turn take their name from Henry VIII's Citadel, which had two impressive towers that the designer of the law courts copied. Carlisle station was designed by William Tite in 1847 for the Lancaster & Carlisle and Caledonian Railways. One can only dream of standing on the platform with a modern camera and a plentiful supply of colour film as, pre-1923, the station was used by seven different companies, all in different colours, from blue to black and everything in between. The brakes are squealing and we come to a halt. This time we make a steady exodus as I think we are all feeling tired. After a last few photographs we shall make our way to a small hotel we have booked in to. We have enjoyed our journeys, as I hope you, the reader have. Here's to our next journey!

'Royal Scot' no. 46118 *Welch Fusilier* coasts into Carlisle station.